THE ALMOST GOSPEL

DRAB TOAD

Copyright © 2025 by Drab Toad.

All rights reserved.

Published by – Notion Press in March, 2025

ISBN: 979-8897771875

The author does not intend to harm, offend, or defame any individual, group, or entity.

Call this not scripture,
but a survival song written backwards.

So, what is this book about?
About everything I once mistook for love.
And what did you find?
That love wasn't supposed to feel like debt.
or drama. or endurance.
What is it then?
The moments I stopped performing.
And the gospel part?
That there was still something sacred left…
even in the almost.

The Anatomy of This Gospel

Once, a child asked a wandering poet:
"Where do all the love poems go when the love
ends?"

The poet knelt beside him and answered,
"They don't go anywhere. They stay.
Some become ruins.
Some become roots.
And the bravest ones, they become scripture."

This book is made of those brave ones.
Not because they know the truth,
but because they dared to almost
name it.

SECTION 1

I've met brilliance before.
I've known kindness, I've seen beauty,
I've admired strength,
separately, in fragments.
But never all at once,
never without contradiction.
Until her.

She didn't interrupt my life.
She tuned it.
As if all the dissonance I once called
solitude was simply waiting
for someone to walk in and make sense
of the notes.

She did not make an entrance,
she became an axis.
An anchored gravity I could orbit without
needing to be pulled.
She was not the storm that changed me.
She was the pause that made me realize
I had survived too many.

There was no lesson in her presence.
Only memory,
as though I had once known her
in the buried original of some older self
before I even had words to name
the pull of the unnamed.

She is not perfect.
But she is precise.
Nothing in her exists by accident.
Even her silence is shaped with intention.

She didn't demand devotion.
She made it feel inevitable.
Not because she asked to be honored,
but because your soul stands straighter
in her presence,
like a sanctum built from breath just to
hold her grace.

You don't worship her.
You walk beside her,
and in doing so,

you remember who you were before the
world convinced you to shrink.

She is the kind of woman
that poets don't exaggerate,
they fall short trying.
Because every line they've ever written
was only rehearsal for the moment she
entered the room.

If you ever see me become someone I
wasn't before,
if my language changes,
if my silences deepen,
if my metaphors finally learn their place,
know this:

She didn't teach me how to write better.
She gave the words a reason to exist.

She is not the line.
She is the breath that made it necessary.

Before thunder,
before flame,
before time thought to measure itself,
there was the pause
where the cosmos inhaled
before a man speaks
the truth that will fracture him into
meaning.

She arrived not as lightning,
but as the reason it strikes.
Not a storm,
but the sky remembering
why it needed to hold rain.

Every poet had lied until her.
Not out of deceit,
but because
she had not yet been real enough
to require the truth.

You are the language God forgot to write.
You are the syntax of every man
who never knew how to say "more"
without breaking.

Before her,
language was an architecture of fossils,
I wandered its halls,
a tenant of borrowed meaning.
Then, her voice:
not ornament, but ordinance.
A lexicon summoned from certainty,
not suggestion.

She never shaped my tongue,
she forged its purpose.

You are not a force I oppose,
but a theorem
that renders resistance obsolete.
Not submission,
but the inevitable collapse of
contradiction
before an axiom too flawless to dispute.

You do not break the silence.
You are its solvent.

Your presence bends language like light,
each glance a curved clause
no grammar can contain.

I no longer write poems.
I obey them.
They come for you, not from me.
I am only the steward
of your arrival in metaphor.

The sky could never alphabet you.
And yet I try,
because some truths deserve their
failures.

You are not beautiful.
You are the architecture
that taught me how to receive beauty
as inheritance.

Before you,
I mistook symmetry for depth,
a face for a force,
a feeling for a covenant.

But you arrived with contradictions
stitched into your gravity,
fierce and forgiving,
soft-spoken but sovereign.

I saw the divine in you
not because you demanded worship,
but because you needed none.

You carry incompatible virtues
like an impossible harmony,
loyal but untethered,
gentle without apology,
humble with flame in your chest.

You made my logic sit down.
You made my soul take notes.

You are not a muse.
You are the standard
by which muses are measured.

You arrived like weather,
not to disrupt,
but to remind the earth
of its own shape.

My walls didn't fall,
they bowed.

You are the tempest that teaches
structure,
the rain that writes scripture
across skin
and bruise
and arrival.

She was not dazzling.
She was undeniable.
There are women whose beauty
distracts.
Hers commanded attention,
not by calling for it,
but by being impossible to ignore
without feeling
as though you missed a sacred
appointment.

She didn't beautify space.
She sanctified it.

I knew silence,
until you arrived.

Then, what I once named absence
became a fracture in the frequency,
a static in the chambers of before.

You do not loop.
You resolve.
A frequency tuned past hearing,
felt in the bones of meaning.

You dismantled indifference.
You outlawed inattention.

Now, every breath is a ritual.
I no longer hear,
I attend.

You did not restore my faith in love.
You rewrote my definition of truth.

I had survived on illusions,
easy myths that looked like grace
but spoke like ghosts.

Then you walked in
with nothing performative,
everything prophetic.

You made me unlearn my performances.
You made me inhabit my promise.

Silence was our first dialect,
a lexicon of withheld affirmations
that needed no utterance.

I never chose you,
I recognized you,
as gravity recognizes mass,
as light acknowledges dawn.

Our contract was signed
in the margins of every unsaid word,
notarized by the bone-deep certainty
that some truths transcend testimony.

You will not find her name here.
Because she is not a character,
she is the axis.

She is not idealized.
She is real.
Which is to say:
Unreasonable. Precise. Immovable.

And still, the only reason
I ever let language undo me
and called it love.

It's not insomnia.
It's yearning in the shape of vocabulary.

You are not just inspiration.
You are interruption.
A muse that doesn't knock,
she drafts the door into being.

I write because I don't want to forget
the look in your eyes
when you first realized I saw you.
Not like a metaphor,
but like a meaning.

There was the Vedas,
then the silence between mantras.
Then there was you,
proof that divinity
does not need a temple
when it walks in skin.

You do not speak.
You manifest.

You do not shine.
You instruct light where to fall.

When they ask who taught me to write,
I will say:
"She made it necessary."

You did not edit me,
you unveiled me.
You made me fluent in what I feared,
grateful for what I could not possess.

You are not the poem.
You are the precedent.

The poets will call it madness.
I call it literacy.

I searched for the first line
God ever wrote,
but then I met her,
and realized, he wasn't writing scripture.
He was practicing for her arrival.

SECTION 2

Not all strength roars.
Some holds the silence steady so she
can sing.

"Let her rise."
No.
Let yourself rise into the kind of man
who never asks her not to.

They told him strength was how much
weight he could carry.
But no one taught him that sometimes,
strength is how much space you can
hold,
for someone else to grow.

He didn't interrupt her expansion.
He didn't mistake her confidence for
challenge,
her voice for volume,
her clarity for combat.

He watched her rise
like morning light across his bones,
not to eclipse him,
but to include him
in a sky neither could have filled alone.

She did not need his permission,
but he offered his presence.
She did not ask to be smaller,
and he never demanded it.

This is what a man becomes
when he forgets how to fear her power:
a harbor,
not a leash.
A root system,
not a rope.

She did not want a leader.
She wanted a mirror,
one unshaken by her strength.

He walked beside her,
not ahead, not behind,
but in alignment.
Even when their frequencies diverged,
they shared a direction.

She wasn't asking for balance
measured by symmetry,
but equilibrium held by trust.

He didn't need her softer,
contained,
smaller.
He only needed her whole.
And in that wholeness,
he found his own,
not threatened,
but completed.

Together, they built a life
where no one bowed,
but both belonged.

His voice did not remain in rooms,
but his presence did.

He did not raise his voice to lead.
He lowered his defenses to understand.
He listened
not as an obligation,
but as devotion.

When she spoke,
he absorbed,
not corrected.
And when she needed room,
he widened the walls
without reminding her he built them.

Power is not a volume.
It's a vibration.

And he vibrated with a gravitational
poise that made her brave.

He was never her sculptor.
She did not enter his life to be reshaped.

She came whole.
And he,
he was the one who kept the fire burning
while she molded her own form in it.

He did not mold her.
He molded space.

This is stewardship,
not the crafting of her shape,
but the guardianship of her sanctum.

He was not the artist of her rise.
He was the keeper of the kiln
that kept her becoming lit.

He never asked for less of her.
He only became more himself to meet it.

There was no need for conquering.
No battle to win.

When she succeeded,
he didn't shrink.
He expanded,
into a man who understood
that partnership is not performance.

Her win was not his loss.
It was their crescendo.

And when she was applauded,
he didn't step forward.
He stepped back,
not into shadow,
but into alignment.

Love is not a war.
It's a recognition:
"I will not diminish you
to feel like more of me."

There was weight to him,
not heaviness,
but gravity.

She knew she was free to fly,
but she also knew
where to land.

He didn't raise his voice,
but when he spoke,
the room bent toward clarity.

His masculinity was never loud,
because depth doesn't need a
microphone.

And in that steadiness,
she opened.
Not because he demanded it,
but because the roots he grew
were wide enough to catch her fall
and deep enough to fuel her rise.

She didn't arrive perfect.
She arrived willing.

And he,
instead of holding her to past versions,
blessed each one she evolved into.

He didn't archive her.
He anointed her.
Every becoming was a benediction
he welcomed with a hallowed ease,
the kind that steadied rather than
sanctified.

He didn't ask for yesterday's softness.
He bowed to today's strength.

And when she found new heights,
he offered only one thing:

"More."

He did not possess her.
He contained her the way
a sky contains stars,
not by capturing their light,
but by holding its infinite permission.

He didn't fear her fullness.
He made room for it.

No cages.
No corners.
Just the expanse of a man
so self-anchored
that he could cradle her chaos
without making it about himself.

And when she shined,
he did not need to match her glow,
he simply reflected it.

He didn't ask for credit.
He asked, "Did I help?"

He didn't tether her to his presence,
he built a life where she could fly
and know the ground would still be warm
if she ever returned.

This is not absence.
It's unconditional tethering.

Legacy is not what we hold.
It's what we set free
and still call sacred.

And when she soared,
he didn't chase,
he blessed the wind behind her.

She did not want a throne.
She wanted a room
where both voices
could shape the air with equal weight.

He didn't fear being wrong.
He feared silence
where her truth should live.

He invited her clarity
like rainfall,
knowing sometimes it would flood,
but it would always cleanse.

They didn't agree on everything.
But they agreed on this:
 "Your rise will never cost me mine."

And in that truth,
they both stood taller.

Power does not interrupt.
It listens,
then shapes.

He did not direct her.
He dialogued with her.
Their dreams did not compete,
they composed.

She was not his reflection.
She was a sovereign voice
he chose to harmonize with.

Real power isn't displayed.
It's articulated.
It flows in the way he asks,
not assumes.

It's seen in the silence he leaves
for her words to arrive.

She was never his to build.
He simply learned to stop
getting in the way.

They rose,
not in roles,
but in mutual becoming.

He did not apologize for being soft,
and she did not apologize for being
strong.

They unlearned performance.
They unstitched hierarchy.
They walked forward as sovereigns
who built their own sky.

She did not need his permission.
But when he insisted, she rise,
not because he lacked,
but because he believed,
they both became legend.

Not because of titles.
But because of trust.

Let it be written:
He never stood in front of her brilliance,
never above it,
never behind it.

He stood beside it.
And by doing nothing to obstruct it,
he became a rare kind of man:
a companion, not a competitor.

He rose, not to outshine,
but to walk alongside.

And in that walk,
both were seen clearer.

Both rose higher.

And no one had to shrink for it.

SECTION 3

This isn't a reclamation. It's a return.

A return to something we once knew
before power got confused with
purpose.
Before love started sounding like orders,
before masculinity meant silence,
and femininity meant softness only.

We unlearned a lot here.

We stopped assuming it's her job to
make the house a home,
to remember the birthdays,
to clean the fridge,
to apologize first,
to shrink to keep the peace.

We stopped assuming it's his job to fix
the bulb,
to know all the answers,
to carry every unspoken weight,

to protect without being asked.

And we started seeing the simplest
thing:
Paying bills is not a masculine trait.
Cooking dinner is not feminine.
These are life skills, not roles.

Love is not a delegation.
It's co-creation.
It's doing the work when the other is
tired.
It's doing it even when no one notices.

This isn't about switching the hierarchy.
It's about retiring it altogether.

When we took off the crowns,
we could finally hold hands.

You don't have to be the leader
to be strong.
You just have to be present.

It was never love,
what wore the robe and held the sceptre.
It was order,
dressed in affection's costume.

The throne wasn't forged from trust,
but from expectation,
the kind passed down
like a blood-soaked heirloom,
disguised as devotion.

I called it protection.
You called it compromise.
But cloaked in the velvet of my voice,
was the hunger to be obeyed.

I wore my care like decree.
I disguised control as clarity.
And you, regal in your composure,
dared to bow to nothing but your own
truth.

That was the first crack in the empire,
when your silence
refused to kneel.

I thought power meant being needed.
But you didn't need me.
You chose me.

And that,
was the first time I tasted
a love not dressed in conquest
but in equal flame.

Let it be said:
I removed my crown.
Not because it was stolen,
but because I saw the weight it placed
on your back
and mistook it for embrace.

Let it be said:
This is not surrender.
This is resurrection.
The end of the throne
is the beginning of us.

If love must bow, let both bow,
to the bond, not each other.

There was a time
we measured closeness
in obedience.

A time when love spoke in symphony,
of one voice only,
the louder one.

But I remember the first time
you didn't ask for permission
to be whole.

And I remember
how something in me,
not threatened, but disarmed,
began to soften.

There was no argument that night.
No storm.
Just the silence of a wall unbuilt.

You didn't walk behind me.
You didn't walk ahead.
You stood beside me
like the road itself.

And it occurred to me,
love isn't a crown
one wears better.

It's a balance
we must learn to hold
in shared hands.

So, let's lose the lineage of rulers and
ruled.
Let's forget who leads.

There is no kingdom between us,
only the field.

Only the invitation
to walk in step
without stepping over.

We kept confusing ascent
with hierarchy.

Believing that to rise,
one must first stand
above someone else.

But you taught me
to rise differently.

Not like a flag,
claimed and saluted.

But like the tide,
silent, sure,
bringing all boats with it.

You weren't below me.
You were behind me
when I stumbled,
beside me when I learned.

And when I tried to drag you up
as if from some lesser ground,
you looked at me,

not in refusal,
but in knowing.

You didn't want my crown.
You didn't want to rule beside me.

You wanted us both
unburdened of inheritances
not ours to carry.

Now we rise together,
not in stature,
but in depth.

Our inheritance:
blueprints for battlements,
legends where love
always knelt before power.

They never taught us
how cold the jewels grow
against a pulse-point.
How rule is just fear
in ceremonial armor.
How every "Majesty"
is really a sentence.

You crossed my moat
carrying no banners,
only a question:
What if the walls became trellises?

So, we unbuilt:
each stone removed
became a stepping-stone.
The great hall now houses
the laughter that never asked to leave.
The treasury?
Just a vault for storing sunlight.

In the absence of decrees,
we learned dialect.

The kingdom persists
solely as the shadow
cast by our shared silhouette.

No lineage.
No crest.
Just two pilgrims
and the slow, sweet erosion
of all we were told to cherish.

I wore the crown
before I knew its weight.

Inherited from silences,
forged in gestures never questioned,
doors opened, voices louder,
always being the first to decide
because that's what men do.

You never asked me to remove it.
But you never bowed.

And that was the miracle.

You made me realize
it wasn't power I was carrying,
it was distance.

The crown did not make me noble.
It made me unreachable.

So, I placed it down
between us.

Not as an offering,

but as an apology.

And you,
you didn't touch it.
You touched me.

There's a difference
between being held up
and being held.
You didn't need to be placed
on any higher place
to shine.

You were already luminous.
Already whole.

My job was not to elevate you.
It was to make space
for the wind behind your choices.

Not to hold you frozen in grace,
but to steady you
so, you could move.

Let me not be your pedestal.
Let me be the ground
you don't have to look down from.

Let me be the steady
from which your storms
take flight.

We used to speak
in instructions.

"I'll protect you."
"You'll follow me."
"This is how it works."

Until we began speaking
in questions.

"Do you feel seen?"
"Can we try again?"
"What do you need?"

And suddenly,
love began to sound less
like war strategy
and more like music.

No commands.
No rewards.

Just pulse.
And pause.
And the space

where nothing needed proving
between notes.

We no longer speak to each other
like generals.

We speak
like composers.

You taught me
that strength
isn't always loud.
It isn't the raised voice.
The final word.
The last say.

Sometimes, strength
is a man washing the dishes
while she undoes the day.

Sometimes, it's listening
without formulating a reply.

Sometimes, it's letting her cry
without trying to fix the storm.

I used to think love was a podium.
Now I know
it's what you do
when no one's watching.

Power, it turns out,
doesn't need a platform.
It just needs presence.

He washed the dishes without being
asked.
Not once, but every night that week.
Not because she couldn't.
Not to earn a compliment.
But because her silence was heavier
than usual, and he'd learned, finally,
that love is not asking what's wrong.
It's stepping in where things are hurting.

Sometimes, power is doing the chore without needing applause.

You can't dismantle a throne
while wearing the robe.

You can't claim equality
with clenched fists.

You asked me once,
"What are you willing to shed
to truly stand with me?"

The answer came slowly.
Not in speeches.
But in leaving behind
the armor of expectations.

I shed the need to lead.
To decide.
To always be right.
I shed the fear of seeming small
if you stood tall.

And when I stood before you, bare,
no emblems, no titles,
you didn't mock the nakedness.
You met it.

What if love
wasn't about devotion
to each other,

but about devotion
to what we create
together?

What if we are not
each other's possessions,
but co-creators?

Not rulers.
Not subjects.
Sovereigns of the same soil.

Not bound by duty,
but drawn by resonance.

If I kneel,
it's not because you demand it.

It's because recognition
sometimes looks like gratitude
in a posture.

She doesn't need to be told
how to be soft.

He doesn't need to be told
how to be strong.

They need only be seen,
as breathing things,
not roles cast by tradition.

Our love does not instruct.
It witnesses.
It learns.

You don't teach someone how to shine.
You remove what's blocking the light.

We are not co-authors
because of how we fit.

We are witnesses of becoming
because of how we stay
when it no longer fits,
and we evolve.

She got the promotion.
He packed her lunch.
She was invited to speak.
He stood in the wings, holding her coat.
And no one clapped for him.
That's what made it his version of
showing up.

So, this is it.

No reign.
No crown.
No pretense.

Just us.

We've burned the tapes
that told us who to be.
We've buried the language
of ownership and rank.

Now, there is only
the wild wonder
of two uncaged hearts
choosing.

Not commanding.
Not compromising.

Choosing.

Every day,
every moment,

again.

And in that choosing,
we've found something
more sacred than power.

We've found
partnership.

May the throne rest in peace,
Not in bitterness, but in clarity.
It raised men who didn't know how to
cry.
It raised women who forgot how to rest.
It taught us how to perform,
not how to partner.
And though we wore it with pride once,
We now build something lighter.
Something we don't have to climb into or
down from.
Something we can live in, equally.

This isn't a lecture.
It's a liberation.

You don't need to take a side in love.
You take a seat, beside them.
You wipe the counters together.
You raise each other's standards.
You let go of outdated codes and ask:
what feels true now?

Here's the real redefinition:
Loving each other in ways the world
hasn't taught you yet.

The throne is gone.
And somehow, love feels more royal than
ever.

SECTION 4

The strongest love has no winner,
because it never hosted a war.

We used to grip
like two opposing magnets
mistaking resistance
for connection,
each touch a test of endurance,
each embrace a silent contest.

Then, the friction dissolved.

Not from fatigue,
but from mutual understanding
that some bonds strengthen
when released.

Now, we orbit
without gravity's insistence.

No ledger.
No contest.
Just the unhurried expansion
of what was always there
beyond the struggle,
a field, vast and unmeasured,
where touch is no longer a test
but proof.

Her silence was never empty,
it was a temple of listening
built between our breaths,
each stone placed
with deliberate hands.

I learned to walk its aisles
without asking it to answer back.
To let the stained glass of her poise
disguised as silence
color my impulses
into something softer.

This is how we unlearned performance:
Not by trading scripted selves,
but by mastering the practice
of listening,
where comprehension
becomes its own language,
and every mute moment
a sacrament.

We no longer count:
who texted first,
who apologized last,
who needed more.

Now we marvel at how the fire warms
both sides.

There's no tally in devotion.
Only breath, met by breath,
rising into something we no longer have
to name.

Every time you count, you subtract.

There are no generals here.
No queens. No pawns.

Just two minds
building a language with no war
metaphors,
two hearts
constructing shelter out of laughter,
two bodies
that seek no conquest,
only communion.

What good is a crown if there's no
kingdom left to come home to?

Love gave us no manual.
Only patterns of others' wounds.

So, we lit a match to their rules,
and rewrote our own:
No "you always."
No "I never."

Just "we try."
And "we choose again."
And "we stay awake when the other
forgets how to dream."

She never handed me a role.
She handed me a mirror.

And in it, I wasn't a leader.
I wasn't a protector.
I wasn't a man playing at purpose.

I was just,
honest.

And that,
she said,
was always enough.

We stopped speaking love,
and began being it.

In how I made tea before she asked.
In how she left the door open
when I needed a silence
I didn't need to explain.

We became fluent
in the dialect of consideration.

No declarations.
Just daily rituals of noticing.

We took the doors off every room in our
hearts.

Not for exposure,
but so, there'd be no hiding.

Now,
even our disagreements are sacred,
not because we avoid them,
but because we let them finish teaching
before we interrupt.

Love used to be a line I tried to stay
ahead of.

With her,
it's a circle.

We orbit what matters.
We pass the center back and forth.
Sometimes I lead.
Sometimes she does.
And sometimes we both let go,

just to see where the wind takes us.

We don't take turns shining.
We light each other up without asking
when our turn is.

And when she wins,
I don't shrink.
I illuminate more of her.

Because partnership is never a stage.
It's a lantern passed between
open hands.

They told me strength was being stoic.
They told her softness was surrender.

We redrew the blueprint
by stepping into the middle,
no masks, no shrinking,
just love without ledger.

Our love wears no armor.
That's its magic,
we're still unhurt.

We stopped tending to love like it was a
crop, always measuring growth,
tracking yield.

Now,
it's a wild garden:
sun-warmed,
moon-fed,
never trimmed for performance.

It grows best
when we let it surprise us.

We often mistake equality for symmetry.
But love doesn't need sameness.

It needs sincerity.

Not one giving 50% and waiting for the
match, but each giving their fullness,
even when that fullness looks different.

This isn't about undoing roles, it's about
undoing rivalry.
Not co-dependency.
Not sacrifice in disguise.
But two people who've given up the
scoreboard, and gained a sanctuary.

We were never meant to conquer love.
We were meant to co-compose it.

And sometimes,
the most radical thing you can do in a
world of hustle and hierarchy
is to love someone:

in ways without ritual or permission

in ways the old stories couldn't name

in ways against the blueprint of
transaction

in ways with nothing owed and
everything offered

in ways like soil tending a seed it may
never see

in ways where no currency existed

in ways under the radar of reward

in ways with the kind of care that doesn't
brand itself

in ways as if love were abundance, not
audition, even if no one's keeping track.

SECTION 5

She didn't need foreplay.
She needed to be understood.
Not unzipped like a conquest,
but unbuttoned like a story,
slowly, like decoding a silence, not
cracking a lock,
as if each fold of her body were a secret
she'd forgotten how to trust anyone with.

And he?
He didn't arrive hungry, he arrived fluent.
Not in technique, but in timing.
In the language of breathing slower
when the world demanded speed.
In knowing the difference between
touching and tending.
In waiting for her body to open not from
pressure, but from peace.

It's what happens when a man's desire
becomes a form of literacy,

when he stops asking, "What do you
want?"
and starts listening to what the back of
her knee tells the truth no tongue could
say when he kisses the base of her spine.

It's not just what he does to her.
It's what he undoes.
The shame. The scripts. The suspicion of
slowness.
The world taught her to brace.
He taught her to believe.

And in return, she didn't bloom.
She blessed.

She spoke in arch and tension
slow to name itself
with a grammar his hands memorized,
and in the end,
they weren't bodies anymore,
they were a language
no one else was fluent in,
writing themselves undefinable,
but felt without once saying the word.

The most sacred thing you can do is
touch someone
like they are already whole.

Before his hands found their way,
he paused,
not out of hesitation,
but ceremony.

As if her skin held scripture
and he had come unworthy,
barefoot at the edge
of everything he had to unlearn.

The air between them
wasn't silent,
it was breathing.
A slow incantation
spoken in the breath
between longing
and permission.

He didn't reach.
He listened.
To the way her breath
tightened the hour,
to the way her pulse
offered a benediction.

She was not a thing to begin,
she was already becoming.
He merely knelt
at the edge of her becoming
and waited for her to open
the sanctum of her consent.

Not like a door.
Like a dawn.

He never asked her
what she liked.
He studied her
until the question became irrelevant.

Every syllable of unsaid intention,
every subtle withdrawal,
every breath that stuttered like
a melody made of hesitation,
he learned them all
like a foreign language
worth mastering
without ever needing to speak.

He wrote poems with the flat of his
tongue,
syntax made of surrender,
and commas came in gasps.

Not performance.
Not conquest.
But correspondence,
between her blood's permission
and his attunement in receiving it.

When he kissed her,
it was not to make her feel beautiful.
It was to remind her:
she was divine before he arrived,
he only illuminated
what was already sanctified.

His hands didn't claim.
They translated.

The skin remembers
who touched it with care,
and who only reached to conquer.

She never mapped her wounds,
he simply learned to navigate
by the stars of her scars,
each constellation unfolding
its own fractured history.

There was no choreography,
only consecration.

He didn't undress her.
He peeled back timelines,
undoing centuries of shame
with fingertips that knew
how to meet without mastery.
how to honor without interruption.

She wasn't aroused.
She was remembered,
as if every inch of her body
had once been a scripture
and he the lost monk
finally fluent in her tongue.

There are gospels
that aren't written in ink
but in sighs,
passed mouth to mouth
like sacred breathwork.

He never worshipped her beauty.
He worshipped her awareness,
how she met his devotion
without performance.

He treated her body
as if it were a temple of thresholds
whose stained glass
was made of bruises and blush.

And when she came,
it wasn't noise.
It was light
flooding through
a window finally opened.

He didn't arrive to consume her.
He came to kneel.

Not at her feet,
but at her center,
where her knowing lived.

She'd been worshipped before
by men who thought intimacy
meant hunger.

But he fed her differently,
through pauses,
through the symphony of patience,
through questions asked in breath
and answered in spine.

She was not decoration.
She was axiom.
She was a living gospel.
And every night with him
felt like retranslation,
not into smaller truths,
but into ones
that only bodies can understand.

He never claimed her,
he was allowed in,
the way dawn is permitted
to cross a windowsill
only after proving
it won't shatter the glass.

Not a conquest,
but a conditional grace,
the sort that arrives
when you've unlearned
how to knock.

She opened to him
like vellum opens to light:
not to be rewritten,
but to reveal gold leaf
hidden between the lines.

Her consent wasn't given,
it resonated,
vibrating through his bones
until his hands understood
their new alphabet:

Where silence meant listen deeper.
Where tenderness was the blade
that carved his old hunger
into grace that asked no return,
a devotion shaped without demand.

He drank from her
as from an ancient well,
not to quench thirst
but to learn what water
remembers.

Every brush of lips
posed new inquiries:
What does this curve
know about gravity?
How does that pocket of breath
define absence?

She answered in
a dialect of bone-memory,
not with solutions,
but with older,
better questions.

In the end,
they didn't find answers.
They discovered
the sacred syntax
that exists
between question

and response,
where all true
conversation begins.

She once believed
the divine was distant.
That untouchable lived above.
Until he reminded her,
grace prays without sound
in the way her hips remember home.

He didn't teach her new things.
He unburied old ones.

Her breath became a prayer pressed into
pulse.
Her thighs, the prologue to divinity.
Her back arching like resurrection
made flesh.

She wasn't sinful.
She was a gospel
written in her own tongue,
never needing salvation,
only space.

He followed her pulse
like monks follow bells,
not to control time,
but to enter it.

Not an explorer.
Not a master.
He was a translator
of syllables only presence could hear
just under the silence
she wore like armor.

He didn't seduce.
He served.

And the moment she came undone,
he didn't claim it.
He received it,
like a blessing
only the faithful understand.

He did not arrive to solve her.
He arrived to be solved by her.

She did not make sense
in categories or positions.
She made meaning
only in presence.

He touched her
like punctuation touches poetry,
not to finish the line,
but to help it breathe.

And in return,
she opened like an answer
to a question
he forgot he was asking.

Touch her like the future depends on it.
Because maybe it does.

They didn't need candlelight.
Or words.
Or the right playlist.

He worshipped her
on an ordinary Tuesday
like men pray before sleep,
not out of duty,
but because something in him
felt held.

She didn't need lace.
She needed honesty.

And his lips,
slow with knowing,
became the ground
where masks dissolved,
where neither of them
had to pretend.

The lips that speak slow are the ones she listens to most.

When it ended,
there was no grief.
Only gratitude
for the kind of love
that teaches the body
it was never a battleground.

He left her
not emptier,
but fuller,
like rain leaves the soil richer
even when the clouds move on.

Their bodies had spoken
without performance,
without apology,
just pure, sacred fluency.

And maybe that's all
the divinity ever wanted:
to be felt
without being named.

No climax is worth chasing if it costs clarity.

There's a difference between being bare
and being seen.
The former is exposed.
The latter is witnessed.

And that's what this was.

Not climax, but communion.
Not seduction, but translation.
Not friction, but the collapse of two skins
who remembered,
oh,
they were once soul.

This wasn't performance.
This was a pilgrimage.
He didn't earn her body,
he earned silence between her gasps.
He earned the soft rupture of letting go,
not from speed,
not from urgency,
but from surrender.

We have cheapened the sacred
by confusing loudness with passion.

But the deepest things in the world
arrive the way dusk enters a room,
like tears down cheeks that never learned
what it meant to be kissed
without bracing for impact.

So, let it be this:

Devotion isn't always gentle.
But it is never careless.

Let your mouth remember it can be
a devotion disguised as breath.
Let your fingers forget everything they were told,
and learn again how to listen.

Let your skin not rush to be touched,
but to be read.

SECTION 6

There comes a love that doesn't just stir
your heart, it dismantles your gravity.

The kind that doesn't happen in one
confession or moment.
It happens in the patient undoing of your
reasons.
It doesn't "begin", it reveals.
And by the time you notice,
you are no longer who you were.

This isn't the love they told you to look
for.
Not the one with a list or a label or a
linear arc.
It's the one you stopped believing in
because it didn't make sense.
Because it asked for the part of you
no one had ever reached.

It's not about chemistry, or compatibility,
or closeness.

It's about collapse.
The collapse of what love used to mean,
the surrender of what it never needed to
be.

You don't fall into it.
You disintegrate.
You forget the myths.
You remember yourself.

You look at them, and there's no
metaphor strong enough,
not because it's beyond language,
but because it is language.

It's the soul's mother tongue
finally spoken aloud again.

This is not a moment.
This is the spinal cord of the book.
The pulse braided through every earlier
page.
The part of you that knew
before you knew.

And if you've ever felt something
too vast for promises,
too intimate for display,
too sacred for symmetry,

then you've been here before.

You just didn't know what to call it.

Before names,
before memory dressed in skin,
there was a promise.

Not spoken.
Not signed.
Just understood in the bones of the
unsaid.

It wasn't about meeting.
You weren't found.
You were remembered.

I didn't fall in love with you.
I fell back into alignment.
As if you were the axis
around which my earliest silence
had always turned.

Some say love rewrites you,
but this,
this winnowed the noise from the
knowing,
till only the original script remained.

Now I know:
you are not a chapter.
You are the spine the book was built
around.

There was a before, you could mark it
with days.
But the after?
It has no border.

Since you,
time has no direction,
distance has no authority,
and place became irrelevant.

I can no longer tell where I am
without checking if you feel it too.

You didn't enter my life,
you restructured the constellations.
You erased North
and said:
Be open. Turn inward. That's where I am.

Long before breath,
we signed something.

Not in ink,
in gravity.

A cosmic contract:
I will forget you
so, I can find you again
and believe in love a second time.

It wasn't about fate.
It was about fidelity
to a reunion we couldn't explain
but always honored.

You were never new.
You were always the prayer
I carried without sound,
but kept living toward.

You didn't hold me.
You undid me.

Not with touch,
but with clarity.

Each moment in your presence
was melting of myth,
of story,
of wound,
of architecture.

Not love as building.
Love as collapse,
until nothing remained
but the self
that could finally stay.

Some loves don't complete you.
They collapse the illusion that you were
ever broken.

Before you, I chased.
After you, I listened.

Not to sound,
but to the exhale
I didn't know I was holding.

You ended the idea
that love was something to reach.

It became something
that reached through me,
wordless,
formless,
but utterly mine.

I stopped hungering
because you were not fulfillment.
You were the exit
from needing to be full.

There are mirrors that show you
your face.
You are not that.

You are the mirror
that showed me
where my form
had been pretending to be me.

You didn't reflect me.
You revealed me.
And every part of me
that couldn't be named
suddenly had a witness.

Not because you saw me,
but because you never asked me
to explain.

You don't meet them.
You meet yourself in their gaze.

Every axis has a center.
Unshaken.
Unmoving.
Undeniable.

That's what you are,
not the spin,
but the truth the spin makes visible.

The silence that holds the storm.

Before you,
everything in me was reaction.
With you,
everything became response.

There is a home behind the breath
in all of us.
You are what reminded mine
to return.

There's a direction that doesn't face out.

It's not East or forgiveness.
Not North or progress.

It's called truthward.
It's the way I face when I think of you.

Not because you are truth,
but because you point me there.
Effortlessly.
As if truth only ever needed one voice
to sound like home.

And you were that voice
before you ever spoke.

Not every home has walls.
Some have frequencies.

I used to map the world
with a desperation to arrive.

But every time I held your gaze,
the cartography of desire
crumbled.

No more needing to be found.
No more coordinates.

You are the place.
Not a destination,
but a dimension.

I didn't arrive at you,
I vanished into the self
that no longer needed to escape.

It wasn't deja vu.
It was recognition.
Like my body had always remembered
what my logic refused to allow.

Not "I know you."
But:
I've always been held by you.

Every past life,
every almost,
led here.

Where memory doesn't follow time
but soulprint.

And mine
has always carried your thumb.

I never wanted to lose myself.
But when I did,
I found that I hadn't vanished.
I had arrived.

You weren't the merger.
You were the permission.

You didn't break my borders.
You reminded me
they were never real.

Love didn't absorb me.
It aligned me
with the version of me
that was never afraid to disappear.

You were never the whirlwind.
You were the axis it circled.

Everything that fell apart
wasn't chaos,
it was choreography
making room for meaning.

And when it all forgot how to spin,
when the axis settled,
there you were.
Not as prize.
Not as proof.
But as presence.

The final truth:
Love doesn't orbit us.
We are the spin love makes sacred.

After all the metaphors fail,
after the questions run out of asking,
after the ego has exhausted every theory
of love,
there is only this:

A wordless recognition.
A presence you don't chase.
A knowing so rooted, it humbles the want
that came before words.

This love is not the climax.
It's not the crescendo.
It's the tuning fork that tells you what
pitch your soul was always meant to sing
in.

It doesn't arrive to rescue or to refine.
It simply is,
and you become real beside it.

There are no chants to make it real.
No rituals.
No proof.

Only that undeniable inner exhale.
The kind that says:

"So, this is what they meant."

And you'll never need to ask again.

SECTION 7

What remains after love isn't absence,
it's everything that had the
courage to stay.

Grief is not an exile; it is a migration.

She said goodbye in silence,
but it unfolded like ancestral myth.
Not in what she said,
but in what she chose not to undo.

You still fold the towel the way
she used to.
Not because it's efficient,
but because that's how she touched
the world.
With precision. With presence.
With a kind of grace that still teaches.

Grief isn't always loud.
Sometimes it's just muscle memory
refusing to forget
how love once lived here.

And you?
You don't miss her voice.
You miss the version of you
that only existed when she called your
name.

You never returned the books.
I never erased your birthday from the
calendar.
There are treaties we never signed,
and yet they govern the way I now walk
through my days.

Love does not always exit by the door.
Sometimes it remains in the hall,
a familiar coat you can't bring yourself to
fold away.

You taught me how to stay.
Which is why I now carry absence
like a rite I was ordained into.

Not because you asked me to,
but because there are covenants too
sacred to dissolve,
even in your leaving.

Your laughter still exists
in the crevice between thoughts.

It shows up in jokes I no longer tell,
in rooms I don't speak in.

I tried to rebuild.
But every new joy knocks on the
unfinished beams
you once made whole.

There's a difference between forgetting
and choosing to carry
what the world no longer asks you to
name.

This isn't a wound.
It's a reverberation.

Most days, I don't feel heavy,
I just notice how often I orbit the things
you touched.

A chair I don't sit in.
A tea I no longer make.
The hesitation before joy,
as if I must ask your ghost for permission
to continue.

Grief doesn't interrupt motion.
It shapes it.

Even when I rise,
I am rising around the gravity of what we
lost.

They say healing is linear.
They say closure is possible.
They say you'll love again, and it will feel
different.

But some memories aren't ghosts,
they're guardians.

Some losses become coordinates,
not to escape, but to return
to where you learned the cost of
meaning.

You didn't leave me broken.
You left me open.
And the world has never stopped
rushing in.

There's no such thing as closure,
only continuance.

You're no longer here,
but the decisions you shaped still ripple.

The way I argue.
The pause before I lie.
The fact that I never, ever forget to say
goodbye.

You've become weightless,
and somehow heavier than ever.

You are not my sorrow.
You are my proof
that something once mattered so much,
its absence reorganized my entire
existence.

Your name still rings in me,
but I no longer rise to meet it.

It's not indifference.
It's integration.

What you left became the root.
And I had to learn
how to distinguish memory from
invitation.

Grief matured into grace.
Not a pull to return,
but a permission to keep what was
without reenacting it.

There was a voicemail she saved.
Not because it was meant for meaning.
Just the way he said her name,
as if it was still his favorite word.

You didn't leave me objects.
You left me heat.

I don't wear your sweater,
I wear your daring.

I don't listen to your favorite song,
I speak with your certainty
when I'm afraid to ask for what I want.

Some loves don't remain in form.
They reappear as courage
when no one's watching.

He left his sweater on the back of a chair.
She never wore it.
But once a month, she'd open the closet
just to make sure it still smelled like him.
When it didn't, she cried,
not because the scent was gone,
but because it meant time had moved
forward
without asking her permission.

You don't haunt me.

You guide me,
even now, especially now,
when I forget how to soften
or when I harden where I once would
have reached.

I keep you not on a shelf,
but in a sentence, I repeat
right before I choose to become kinder.

You weren't the end.
You were the compass
that pointed me back to myself.

What you lost is not behind you,
it became you.

I don't want to rebuild from you.

Let these ruins remain,
each grief-scribed
surface a testament,
each leaning wall
a counterspell
to forgetting's design.

No restoration.
No demolition.
Just this persistent geometry:
floorstones creased
by presence,
rafters still fragrant
with extinct incense.

I am not debris.
I am evidence,
the stubborn preservation
of what gods
no longer visit
but cannot erase.

The ruins are not proof of failure.
They're proof something sacred once
stood here.

They ask why I don't speak of you
anymore.
It's not forgetting.
It's fluency.

You've become a language
I no longer need to pronounce
because I live inside it.

You taught me to speak in silence.
You taught me to stay, even in departure.
You became the syntax of every sacred
boundary
I now offer the world.

I do not write you anymore.
You are the ink.

They'll say I healed.
But what really happened
was I found a way to carry you
without explaining you.

You became loop,
not story.
You became shape,
not object.
You became prayer,
not performance.

And in the barest moments,
when I least expect it,
you rise, not as what used to tremble,
but as architecture.

A grief-scribed ruin.
A devotion-rinsed ruin.
Still grief-lit.
Still tenderproof.
Still here.

We are taught to count love by its
beginnings, its fireworks, its declarations,
its firsts.
But some of the most tenderproof loves
never got to end on their own terms.
And so, they softproof, not to haunt, but
to remind.

The grief-scribed ruin is not what's left
after love fails.
It's what survives when it was real
enough to deserve grieving.

To live after loss is not to forget.
It is to speak in a new dialect,
one where their absence becomes a
compass,
a shadow you now understand
was once light.

You may never be the same.
But that's not a flaw.
That's the inheritance of loving deeply,
of having carried something eternal
in a world not built to hold it.

SECTION 8

We never just become,
we scatter into the versions we dared to
imagine.

In the multiverse, there is a version of us
that never needed closure.

In one timeline,
we argued on the second week,
and instead of leaving,
we unpacked.

You said too much.
I said too little.
But we both stayed long enough
for the silence to find its voice.

There is a version of us
that did not end to protect its perfection,
it grew clumsily, gloriously,
through the mess.

We aged inside it,
not gracefully, but authentically.
And that was the real promise.

Somewhere,
we pass each other at the crosswalk.
Your eyes are kind.
Mine are tired.
We nod, strangers being polite.

But I go home with a ghostglow
I can't explain.
A warmth behind my ribs
with no name.

Even in that world,
you taught me something.
Some souls don't need an exchange
to leave a gracemark.

We ended, yes.
But in that version,
we didn't let the ending be the grave.

Years later,
we met again, older, stranger,
but still fluent in the same language
the world had forgotten.

We weren't romantic anymore.
We were something braver.
Two unwound chords that decided
to speak again.

We didn't last.
But we believed in us so hard
that it built a room inside the universe
that still exists.

Wherever we are,
our dreaming selves
go back there,
at night,
between decisions,
on birthdays we don't remember
sharing.

And maybe that's enough.
Maybe dreaming was the version
we were meant for.

You told me you loved me
when I had nothing left to give.
I told you I was ready
when you were halfway gone.

But we still said it.
We still named it.
And that naming
left an aftermark in the world
neither of us can deny.

Some versions don't bloom.
They just leave perfume on the skin
for years after.

Some loves don't need a timeline.
They just need to be named once, fully.

I wrote letters I never sent.
You paused before dialing my number.
We became fluent in the grammar
of almost.

And somehow,
that near-ness became its own kind of
intimacy.
Not lived, but imagined so vividly,
it taught us both how to love better
in our actual lives.

"She's married now," he says, sipping
slowly.
"Do you still love her?" his friend asks.
He doesn't answer.
But for the first time in weeks,
he checks the weather where she lives.
And that's enough of an answer.

You were not my softest moment.
You were my threshold.

We met when nothing made sense.
We forged each other
like fire forges steel.

That version of us
wasn't tender.
But it was real.

And even if we didn't survive it,
we survived because of it.

In one vein of time,
we became untouchable.

Not because we were perfect,
but because we transcended sequence.
Love, in that space,
wasn't measured by clocks
or calendars.

It simply was.
Like gravity.
Like breath.

And that's the version
the stars still talk about.

We never broke up.
We just... faded.

No fight.
No decision.
Just life folding in other directions.

But even in the silence,
something remains.
Not longing.
Not pain.
Just recognition
that once,
something sacred
chose to rest here.

Even after the last goodbye,
we didn't rot.

We became compost,
feeding the ground
for every love that followed.

You are in my tenderness now.
In the way I listen.
In the way I pause
before reacting.

You didn't stay.
But you never really left.

You were once my anchor.
Now, you're my wind.

You used to hold me steady.
Now you remind me how to drift.

In that version,
we kept re-meeting each other,
in new shapes,
new contexts,
like seasons that forgot
they were supposed to end.

Love didn't stay the same.
But it never stopped arriving.

In one life, they broke up.
In another, they grew old together.
But in every version,
she still keeps his birthday in her
calendar.
Just in case.

Somewhere,
in the overlap of dreams and dusk,
we still hold hands.

We still dance in the kitchen.
Still argue over nothing.
Still apologize too late
and forgive too soon.

That version of us
wasn't fiction.
It was just...
a draft the universe
decided to keep.

Tucked away.
Cherished.
Unpublished,
but whole.

If you've ever missed someone
you never really had,
you understand this fold.

If you've ever mourned an almost,
a maybe,
a mirror-life that slipped away
without anyone doing anything wrong,

you've already visited this place.

We are not failures for the timelines we
didn't live.
We are proof that the heart has more
rooms
than the world has maps.

This was never about wishing.
It was about witnessing,
the infinite configurations
your love could have taken.

And honoring each one
like a language
only the soul understands.

Somewhere,
you and I are still walking toward each
other.
Still unfolding.
Still real,
even if only
in the architecture of possibility.

And maybe that's the version
that saves us.

SECTION 9

We mistook the mirror for the muse,
and called the reflection love.

You didn't break my heart.
I broke it against the idea of you.

I didn't fall in love with you.
I fell in love with what you resembled
when I was tired of asking myself the
harder questions.

You didn't lie.
You simply stood where my longing
needed a shape.
And I draped a story over your silhouette,
one with softer chapters
and a happier ending
than I was ready to write for myself.

That version of you?
She wasn't dishonest.
She was just premature.
She came from the part of me still
learning
what love isn't.

You didn't break my heart.
The myth did.
And it broke exactly where I had built it
too high.

Real love doesn't audition.
It arrives uncostumed.

I mistook it for fate,
that familiar quickening when you
entered.

But it wasn't you I knew.
It was the feeling left behind
by an old hurt,
finally recognizing someone who fit the
silence it created.

You weren't my twin flame.
You were the outline of an old bruise
my body remembered as home.

And I filled you in with hopes
that had nothing to do with you,
only everything to do with the parts of
me, I still thought someone else should
complete.

You didn't audition.
I just cast you.

Gave you lines I wrote in the dark,
costumes tailored from my unmet needs,
a plotline already decided
before you spoke a word.

And when you stumbled over the role,
when you acted like a person instead of
the character I'd created,
I called it disappointment.

But maybe what cracked wasn't love.
It was the stage collapsing
under the weight of my assumptions.

We don't fall in love, we stage it.
Cast them as savior, script their lines
from our hunger...

I said we "clicked."
But what I meant was,
you felt like something I almost survived.

Our magnetism was not magic.
It was muscle memory.
I didn't recognize you from the stars,
I recognized you from the patterns.
The old want. The blueprint of my
wanting.

We called it electricity,
but it was just two old sparks
reigniting a flame
we both used to burn in.
Different name. Same fire.

I loved your potential more than your
presence.
I saw a skeleton of becoming and called
it sanctuary.
I heard your silence and made it soulful.

You never claimed to be what I needed.
But I made you the architecture anyway,
built a house of hope out of half a hello
and spent months praying
to my own projections.

He wasn't the fire, he was the match.
I brought the gasoline.

I didn't just want love.
I wanted salvation.
A hand to lift me from myself
without demanding I look back.

You didn't fail me.
I failed to notice,
no one owes you rescue
just because they smiled like a
lighthouse.

You weren't a lifeboat.
You were a shore I mistook
as promised land.

You didn't break me.
You just reflected the parts
I wasn't ready to face.

My anger?
Wasn't about you.
It was about the truth you wordlessly
carried
that I had no name for.

I handed you a myth
and punished you
for not living up to my imagination.

The rush I called "connection"
was desire auditioning again, hoping this
scene would land.

It wasn't you that thrilled me,
it was the idea of being chosen.
Held. Witnessed.
Filled.

I mistook appetite for alignment,
and wonder for certainty.
It took your exit
for me to realize,
you were the placeholder.
I was the source.

You never promised me the version
I wanted.
But I fed you the script anyway,
highlighted the traits I could praise,
muted the ones
I didn't know how to love.

I wanted you to be the poem
I couldn't write alone.
So, I erased your punctuation,
rewrote your breath pattern,
then grew resentful
when the verse wouldn't sing.

I wasn't in love.
I was in editorial control.

You weren't my soulmate.
You were the dress rehearsal
for what it means to stop performing.

To feel the itch of needing to be wanted,
to watch myself contort into palatable
pieces
just to earn a gaze.

You didn't see me,
and maybe that was the point.
To finally stop relying on reflection
to know I exist.

The most merciful thing I've ever done
was stop mythologizing you.

To let your silence be just that,
not a riddle,
not a test,
not a hidden poetry I needed to unlock.

To allow you your humanity,
without disappointment.
To unclench the lens.
To stop turning your name
into a metaphor
for something
I had to rescue inside myself.

The most courageous love?
Seeing their humanity first, and choosing
it anyway.

You were never meant to carry that
much meaning.
You were a moment.
A mirror.
A merciful mistake.

I loved you for what you revealed,
not about you,
but about how far I still had to go
to recognize myself without costume.

I thank you for not being what I wanted.
You were real enough to break the
dream.
And kind enough not to try to fix what
was never yours to hold.

The last time
I mistook someone for my salvation,
they smiled at me
and it felt like spring.

I wrapped a whole myth around
that moment.
Wrote our future from the way their hand
brushed mine.
Designed a temple of projection based
on the sound of their laugh.

They weren't cruel.
They were simply not what I wrote.

And it took losing that fiction
to remember my life was not a
screenplay.

I don't need a co-star.
I need a witness.
And I've become one, finally,
to my own becoming.

At some point,
even the keeper of the imagined fails to
hold the script.

They'll forget the line you scripted
in your head.
They'll say something too human,
or too honest,
or not poetic enough,
and the illusion will split.

But this is not the tragedy.
This is the threshold.

Because real love doesn't start when the
fantasy blooms.
It begins when the myth dies.

It begins in the sigh after the
disillusionment.
In the silence of realizing that you are not
owed anything,
and neither are they,
except the mercy of being seen
without the cloak of your expectation.

You will still long.
You will still hope.
But now,
you'll do it with both feet on the ground.
With both eyes open.
With your heart unarmed.

And maybe next time,
you won't hand them a costume.

You'll hand them a chair.
And say,
*"Sit. Be whoever you are. If we meet
there, we meet there."*

Not because you've given up on love.
But because you've finally begun to
believe in something stronger,
reality, in all its unshaped,
unscripted glory.

SECTION 10

This is not the space where I teach.
This is the one where I finally admit:
there was never a map. Just choices.
Not a religion. Just presence.

I've kneeled in front of structures made
of ambition, bodies, hopes, illusions.
I've mouthed prayers I didn't believe, just
to feel like I still belonged.
But somewhere between losing people
and finding my breath again,
I stopped seeking salvation and started
listening to my own pulse.

This is not the truth I was taught.
It's the one I lived.
Not tidy, not infallible,
but it held.

This is a museum of unspoken stories:
What I mistook as destiny.
What I rewrote with my bare hands.

What no one could give me.
What I gave anyway.

If you're looking for scripture,
you won't find commandments.
You'll find small, blood-warm lines
of someone who kept showing up
when it would've been easier not to.

So let this be the gospel:
the ordinary made sacred
through the sheer audacity of staying.

Not with prophecy.
Not with perfection.
But with what stayed after everything
else left.

Call it faith, call it pattern recognition,
call it instinct,
we build gospels not from thunder but
from things
that refused to abandon us.

You don't need to believe in miracles
anymore.
You are the miracle that survived all the
doubt.

You used to beg for reasons.
Now you bless the silence that replaced
them.

You don't explain your choices to those
who left early.
You live them fully for those who stayed,
especially yourself.

There are truths
you'll never be able to teach.
Because they weren't meant to be
taught, only embodied.

Some truths don't arrive.
They emerge, slowly, like heat under scar
tissue.

No sacred text ever named you.
And still, you became sacred.

Your laughter never appeared in
divine manuals.
But it saved more days than any
blessing.

You are the unwritten verse.
The proof that divinity doesn't need
endorsement, just presence.

We were learning how to become the
match.

All those dark nights?
They weren't punishment.
They were rehearsals for radiance.

You learned to carry
what most people tried to outrun.
And you did it without applause.

Now you glow like someone who doesn't
need rescuing anymore.

The mistake was thinking you had to
leave yourself to find something
unfabricated.

But the sacred was always in your
ordinary:
The rituals that didn't look impressive,
the choices that looked like giving up
but were really giving in, to truth.

You are the temple now.
Don't dim your flame. Rise.

There's no resurrection without residue.
Some ash stays under your nails.

You were not too much.
You were simply not designed for partial
spaces.

The myth said
you had to shrink to be loved.
Your gospel rewrites that with a single
sentence:
"I will not apologize for being fire-born."

Let them call that arrogance.
You'll call it return.

Not a confession.
Not a plea.
Not a performance.

Just a promise.

"I will stay loyal to the self I keep finding
within every disguise."
"I will not let anyone shame me back into
forgetting."
"I will not need to be seen in order to be
real."

Only misunderstood chapters.
People playing roles they didn't know
they were auditioning for.

You stop demonizing.
You start translating.

Not to excuse.
But to remember that peace is a
language, and you're finally fluent.

You left versions of yourself behind,
thinking the leaving was proof of growth.

But some returns are not regressions.
They are reconciliations.

It is not a crime to come back wiser.
To pick up what you once dropped, not
out of weakness, but readiness.

What I worship now can't be housed in
temples. It breathes with me.

Here.
Now.
Not what might be, or what could've
been.

But what is, when no one is looking.
The way your soul sounds when it stops
auditioning.

This breath is your offering.
And your body, the temple of becoming.

They gave you Eden.
They gave you Exodus.
But they never told you about this life-
shaped middle,

Where nothing burns, nothing parts,
nothing rises.
You just live.

And somehow, it is enough.
Not because it dazzles,
But because it doesn't ask you to vanish.

We weren't mythic. We were ordinary,
and that's what made it sacred.

You don't say "Sacred Yes" to beg for
something.
You say it to claim what you've already
become.

This is your gospel:
Not written in ink,
but carried in your bones.

It will not sell.
It will not convert.
It will not impress.

But it will outlast everything that was
only pretending to be truth.

This book doesn't end. It exhales.
You made it through the myths, the mirrors,
the memories,
not because I showed you the way,
but because part of you already knew.

We don't find truth like a treasure map.
We return to it like muscle memory.
And if nothing else,
I hope this book reminded you
that you were never broken,
only becoming.

The Almost Gospel is yours now.
Not to believe, but to reimagine.
Not to memorize, but to answer with your own.

Let the old blueprints fall.
Let your own breath be the sacred proof.

You are allowed to rewrite everything
you were taught.
You are allowed to be the scripture now.

To those who left,
thank you for giving me space to meet myself.

To those who stayed,
thank you for making the silence feel less like
punishment, and more like prayer.

And to you, reading this,
thank you for staying with your own heart long
enough to finish this page.
You were the audience I didn't know I needed.

If you found even one line that felt like a
mirror, then nothing here was wasted.